ANIMAL KINGDOM CLASSIFICATION

PEACOCKS, PENGUINS & OTHER

BIRDS

By Steve Parker
Content Adviser: Debbie Folkerts, Ph.D., Assistant Professor
of Biological Sciences, Auburn University, Alabama

Science Adviser: Terrence E. Young Jr., M.Ed., M.L.S.,
Jefferson (Louisiana) Public School System

First published in the United States in 2006 by
Compass Point Books
3109 West 50th St., #115
Minneapolis, MN 55410

ANIMAL KINGDOM CLASSIFICATION–BIRDS
was produced by

David West Children's Books
7 Princeton Court
55 Felsham Road
London SW15 1AZ

Designer: Rob Shone
Editors: Gail Bushnell, Nadia Higgins
Page Production: Les Tranby, James Mackey

Visit Compass Point Books on the Internet at
www.compasspointbooks.com
or e-mail your request to
custserv@compasspointbooks.com

Library of Congress Cataloging-in-Publication Data
Parker, Steve.
  Peacocks, penguins, and other birds / by Steve Parker.
    p. cm.—(Animal kingdom classification)
  Includes bibliographical references and index.
  ISBN 0-7565-1251-4 (hardcover)
  1. Birds—Juvenile literature. I. Title. II. Series.
  QL676.2.P366 2005
  598—dc22   2005003812

PHOTO CREDITS :
Abbreviations: t-top, m-middle, b-bottom, r-right,
l-left, c-center.

8t, John and Karen Hollingworth ,U.S. Fish and Wildlife Service; 8mt, FreeStockPhotos.com; 8m, U.S. Fish and Wildlife Service; 9t, Curtis Carley, U.S. Fish and Wildlife Service; 9mr (inset), Glen Smart, U.S. Fish and Wildlife Service; 9bl, Dr. James P. McVey, NOAA Sea Grant Program; 10, Mathew Perry, U.S. Fish and Wildlife Service; 12l, David M. Dennis, Oxford Scientific Films; 13t, John Cancalosi/naturepl.com; 13b, David Clendenen, U.S. Fish and Wildlife Service; 14l, U.S. Fish and Wildlife Service; 14/15, Steve Mascowski, U.S. Fish and Wildlife Service; 15tl, William B. Folsam, NMFS; 15tr, David Clendenen, U.S. Fish and Wildlife Service; 19tr, FreeStockPhotos.com; 19m, Dave Menke, U.S. Fish and Wildlife Service; 19br, Peter Oxford/naturepl.com; 19b, NOAA; 20l, Dietmar Nill/naturepl.com; 20b, Steve Maslowski, U.S. Fish and Wildlife Service; 21tr, U.S Bureau of Land Management; 21bl, Dave Watt/naturepl.com; 23m, FreeStockPhotos.com; 23bl, Dave Menke, U.S. Fish and Wildlife Service; 24bl, Phil Savoi/naturepl.com; 24/25b, David Pike/naturepl.com; 25ml, U.S Bureau of Land Management; 25mr, U.S Bureau of Land Management; 25br, Dave Watts/naturepl.com; 27ml, NOAA; 29tl, Commander Grady Tuell, NOAA Corps; 29tr, U.S. Fish and Wildlife Service; 29bl, David Kjaer/naturepl.com; 31tl, NASA; 31ml, Tim Edwards/naturepl,com; 31bl, U.S.D.A Photo by Larry Rana; 31br, Peter Oxford/naturepl.com; 32/32t, NOAA; 33ml, George Gentry, U.S. Fish and Wildlife Service; 33m, Richard Baetsen, U.S. Fish and Wildlife Service; 33mr, Captain Budd Christman, NOAA Corps; 33b, Doug Allan/naturepl.com; 34bl, Cliff Beittel; 34m, William B. Folsom, NMFS; 35t, Gary M. Stolz, U.S. Fish and Wildlife Service; 36br, Gary M. Stolz, U.S. Fish and Wildlife Service; 36/37, Glen Smart, U.S. Fish and Wildlife Service; 38bl, Dave Menke, U.S. Fish and Wildlife Service; 38br, Friedemann Koster, Oxford Scientific Film; 38/39, Dave Menke. U.S. Fish and Wildlife Service; 39t, 'U.S Bureau of Land Management'; 39m, Dave Menke, U.S. Fish and Wildlife Service; 39ml (inset), Lee Karney, U.S. Fish and Wildlife Service; 39 mr, Lee Karney, U.S. Fish and Wildlife Service; 39bl, Steve Maslowski, U.S. Fish and Wildlife Service; 40tl, FreeStockPhotos.com; 40tr (inset), Stephen Tuttle, U.S. Fish and Wildlife Service; 40bm, Gary M. Stolz, U.S. Fish and Wildlife Service; 40br, U.S Bureau of Land Management'; 41tl, Bruce Davidson/naturepl.com; 41tr, Lynn Llewellyn, U.S. Fish and Wildlife Service; 41m, U.S Bureau of Land Management; 41b, U.S Bureau of Land Management; 42/42, P. Martinkovic, U.S. Fish and Wildlife Service; 43tl, John and Karen Hollingworth, U.S. Fish and Wildlife Service; 43tr, David Clendenen, U.S. Fish and Wildlife Service; 43m (inset), Ron Garrison, U.S. Fish and Wildlife Service/San Diego Zoo; 43bl, John and Karen Hollingworth, U.S. Fish and Wildlife Service; 43br, Luther Goldman, U.S. Fish and Wildlife Service; 45b, Digital Vision.

Every effort has been made to contact copyright holders of any material reproduced in this book. Any omissions will be rectified in subsequent printings if notice is given to the publishers.

Front cover: Little sparrowhawk
Opposite: Great horned owl

ANIMAL KINGDOM CLASSIFICATION

PEACOCKS, PENGUINS & OTHER
BIRDS

Steve Parker

COMPASS POINT BOOKS ✦ MINNEAPOLIS, MINNESOTA

TABLE OF CONTENTS

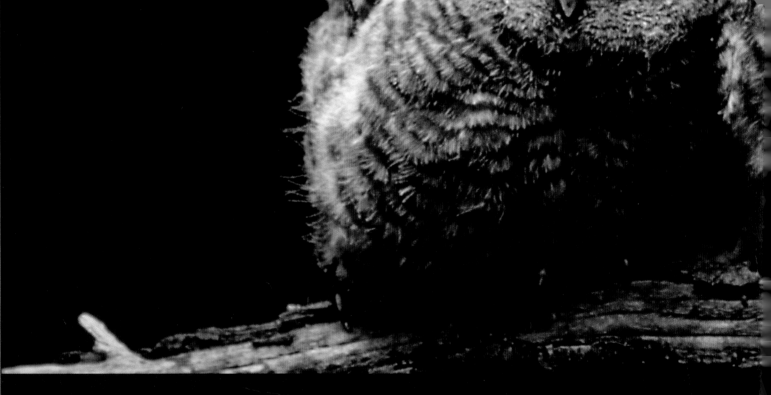

INTRODUCTION

If you look long enough at the sky, you are almost certain to see a bird. These feathered, warm-blooded creatures are the biggest and most expert of all fliers. They live in nearly every part of the world, even the frozen poles and open oceans. And their powers of flight and freedom, envied by many people, mean that birds travel faster and farther during their lives than any other kind of creature.

Birds bring much wonder and fascination to the natural world. We admire the beautiful colors and patterns of their plumage and listen to their immense variety of songs and calls. We can appreciate their building skills as they construct intricate nests. We follow their complicated patterns of behavior as they feed, court, breed, and raise their young. In the countryside, along seashores and riverbanks, and even in city centers, birds are busy with their daily lives—and they greatly enrich our own.

MASTER OF THE AIR

The great egret is one of about 60 species, or kinds, of birds in the heron family. It lives in all warmer parts of the world, near wetlands such as rivers, lakes, and swamps. During flight it curves its neck into an S shape and its legs trail behind. The flight feathers of the wings are fanned out to catch the tiniest currents of warm rising air. This allows the egret to save energy by gliding great distances without flapping.

DIVERSE AND NUMEROUS

There are more than 9,000 species of birds in the world. They occupy every type of living place, or habitat, from dense forests and mountain peaks to remote islands far out at sea. Only the ocean's deeper waters lack birds.

COPING WITH COLD

Birds, like mammals, are warm-blooded. They "burn" energy from their food to keep their bodies constantly warm. As long as they eat enough, birds can stay active even in freezing places, where cold-blooded creatures such as lizards, frogs, and insects could not move.

Flight gives birds an advantage over mammals. They can cover great distances to avoid harsh weather and to locate food, whereas land mammals cover distance more slowly. This is why birds are found farther north and south than any other animals. They soar over the ice of the Arctic and the great frozen landmass of Antarctica.

ON THE MOVE

Flight has similar benefits in warmer habitats, too. In the desert, birds can soar high and scan the landscape for pools of water or sources of food. In forests, they can rise above the trees and reach new feeding grounds quickly. The main drawback of such an active life is that birds need a constant supply of high-energy food. In some habitats, this supply is lacking during the cold or dry season. But again, birds can cope. They stay while conditions are good and then fly away on migration to avoid the harsh season.

NORTHERN FORESTS
Nutcracker

MOUNTAINS
Ptarmigan

GRASSLANDS AND DESERTS
Quail

SOUTHERN POLAR
Penguins

NORTHERN POLAR

Arctic loon

RIVERS AND LAKES

Eurasian kingfisher

TROPICAL FORESTS

Green-billed toucan

OCEANS

Fairy tern

TEMPERATE FORESTS

Barn owl

Some birds are so rare that they are in danger of dying out forever. The forest homes of the Philippine eagle are being cut down for timber and to make way for farmland. This reduces the number of monkeys and forest birds available for eagle's prey. There are probably fewer than 250 of these huge birds left. The most common of all birds is the domestic chicken. It is kept worldwide for eggs and meat, and its numbers are estimated at 10 billion.

Egg-laying chickens (above) and Philippine eagle (inset)

9

BIRD BODIES

A bird body's key features are lightness combined with strength. Plenty of muscle but few heavy body parts make flying more efficient. Inside are most typical animal parts, like those in our own bodies.

SKELETON
Most bones of the skeleton are hollow with air spaces inside to save weight. The sternum (breastbone) has a large, flat keel to anchor the muscles that flap the wings.

Upper leg bone (femur)   Keel   Upper wing bone (humerus)

BODY PLAN
In many ways, birds are typical land vertebrates—animals with backbones. They have an inner skeleton of bones, including a vertebral column or backbone, a skull, four limbs, and a tail. The rear limbs are also typical, with toed feet. But the front limbs are very different—they are wings designed for flight.

FEATHERS
The bird's body covering is very lightweight, keeps in body warmth, and provides color, camouflage, and protection.

DIGESTION
Food is swallowed into a baglike crop for storage. Then it passes to the muscular gizzard, or stomach, and is mashed to a pulp.

Intestines

SAVING WEIGHT
If a female bird like this goose had to carry developing young inside her, as mammals do, she would be too heavy to fly. So she leaves them behind to develop inside eggs in the nest.

Cloaca (opening for wastes and reproduction)

REPRODUCTION
Eggs pass from the ovary, along the oviduct tube, and out through the cloaca.

BRAIN

The brain is large for the body size. The cerebellum coordinates muscles. The optic lobes deal with information from the eyes.

Cerebellum

Cerebrum

Brain stem

Optic lobe

Optic nerve to eye

Smell brain

Skull

Cervical (neck) bones

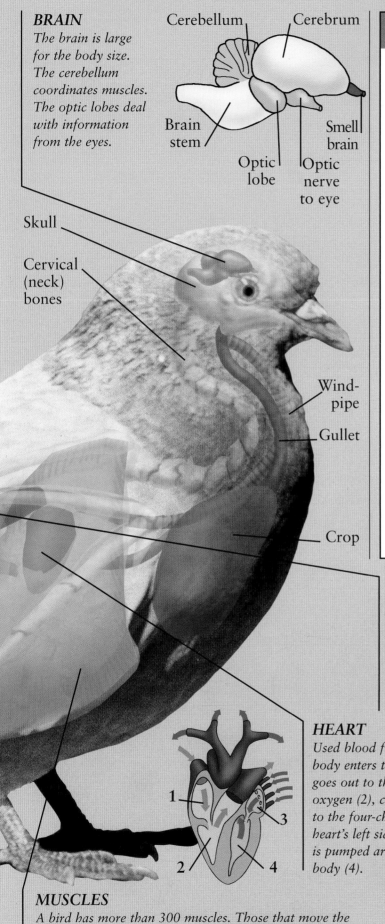

Wind-pipe

Gullet

Crop

FEET AND PERCHING

A few birds have two toes on each foot, a few have three, but most have four. In a woodpecker, two toes point forward and two point backward. The largest group of birds, called the passerines or perching birds, have three forward-pointing toes and one rear-pointing toe per foot. This allows a firm grasp of a twig or other perch. Passerines outnumber all other groups of birds added together and include familiar types such as blackbirds, sparrows, wrens, robins, and warblers.

A perching Cape white eye (a passerine)

LUNGS

Air is pulled through the lungs to nine air sacs, or chambers, some extending into bones. This gives greater flow of oxygen.

Windpipe

Front air sacs

Lungs

Rear air sacs

HEART

Used blood from the body enters the heart (1) goes out to the lungs for oxygen (2), comes back to the four-chambered heart's left side (3), and is pumped around the body (4).

1

2

3

4

MUSCLES

A bird has more than 300 muscles. Those that move the wings can form up to half of the total body weight.

11

ORIGINS OF BIRDS

The first birds probably flew through the air 155 million years ago, in the middle of the Age of Dinosaurs. Those early birds may have descended, or evolved, from small meat-eating dinosaurs.

LOOK OUT!
Gastornis (Diatryma) *lived 40 million years ago. It could not fly, but was a fierce hunter. Here, it is attacking an early type of horse.*

FIRST KNOWN BIRD

The earliest known bird is *Archaeopteryx*, which means "ancient wing." It was about the size of a crow and was covered in feathers. Its front limbs were fully formed wings, but smaller and weaker than most bird wings of today. It had some dinosaurlike features, such as teeth and a long, bony tail, which today's birds lack. *Archaeopteryx* lived in what is now Germany. It could fly, but not as well as modern birds.

AMAZING REMAINS
We know about ancient creatures from their fossils preserved in rocks. This fossil of Archaeopteryx shows its head arched over its back.

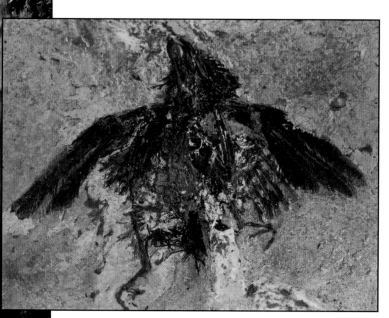

This fossil bird from 45 million years ago shows feathery details.

BIRDS SPREAD OUT

By 65 million years ago, when dinosaurs died out, there were hundreds of kinds of birds. Some were hunters, while others ate fruits and seeds. During the following time period, many kinds of birds came and went. Some have died out only recently and were probably killed off by people. The giant moas of New Zealand stood more than 3 yards (2.7 meters) tall and were still alive just a few hundred years ago.

GIANT OF THE SKIES

The largest flying bird, *Argentavis*, lived about 5 million years ago in what is now Argentina. It weighed 220 pounds (100 kilograms), and its wingspan was more than 8 yards (7.3 m). The biggest fliers today, albatrosses and condors, have wingspans of up to 3 yards (2.7 m).

A condor (left) is half the size of Argentavis, shown compared to a person (below).

FEATHERS AND FLIGHT

Birds are the only living creatures with feathers. These amazing body parts are remarkably tough—yet as light as a feather! A typical bird has several types of feathers, each with a different purpose.

FLAPPING

A barn owl shows the down, or power, stroke that keeps the bird up in the air (below), and the up, or recovery, stroke (below right).

STRUCTURE OF FEATHERS

A feather is made from the same substance that forms a bird's claws, as well as our own hair and nails—keratin. Feathers, like our hairs, are dead and have no feeling. They grow from tiny pits in the bird's skin, called follicles. Most outer feathers have a stiff central rod, called the shaft or quill. Small, flexible branches or barbs stick out from it. Even smaller barbules branch from the barbs. The barbules have tiny hooklike parts that lock together, so the whole feather keeps its smooth shape.

WINGS

The structure of a bird's wings corresponds to the arms or forelegs of other vertebrates. There is an upper arm bone (humerus), two lower arm bones (radius and ulna), and elongated wrist and hand bones. These are moved by large muscles in the shoulder and chest.

FASTEST

The peregrine (right) is the fastest flier—and the fastest of all animals. When it swoops on prey in midair, it exceeds 155 miles (250 kilometers) per hour. Some ducks and geese, such as the spur-winged goose, can reach speeds of 62 miles (100 km) per hour.

TAKEOFF

Smaller birds can take off with a little jump. Larger types, like these American avocets, may need to run into a headwind to gain enough air speed to lift themselves from the ground.

TYPES OF FEATHERS

Flight feathers on the wings are long and stiff, with the barbs and barbules forming a smooth, air-proof surface called the vane. Body, or contour, feathers are shorter and often have fluffed-up bases. Beneath them are down feathers, which are soft and fluffy.

Feathers, left to right: tail, body (contour), primary wing, secondary wing, barbs (inset).

FLIGHT CONTROL

The fingerlike primary feathers at the tips of the wings are fanned for precise steering, as in the Californian condor (above right). The main portion of the wing is covered with secondary feathers. To slow down, the tail feathers are also fanned out widely, as in the black-naped tern (above left).

PREENING

Birds like this pelican use their beaks and toes to straighten and clean their feathers, removing pieces of dirt and pests such as fleas.

WARM OR COOL

Feathers are excellent insulators, keeping in body warmth. On very hot days, each feather can also be lifted by a small muscle at the base, for cooling. Most birds molt twice a year. This is when the old feathers fall out and a new set grows in.

BEAKS, FEET, AND CLAWS

irds have no hands for holding items like food or nest materials. So they use their beaks, and some also use their feet. The size and shape of a bird's beak (bill) give clues about what it eats. Beaks are also used for preening feathers, pecking enemies, and as part of visual displays for breeding.

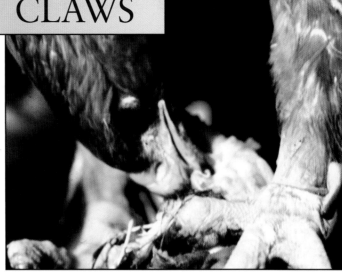

TEARING
An eagle's sharp-edged, hooked beak is ideal for tearing and slicing its victim. It cuts off chunks of meat, which are small enough to swallow.

BEAK STRUCTURE
The beak is a two-part structure made of a hornlike substance that is light yet very strong. The upper part is like a sheath that covers the upper jaw, or mandible. The lower part covers the lower mandible. In birds such as parrots and ducks, the upper beak and the mandible bone inside are not joined firmly to the skull, but attached by a hinge. So the upper beak can move and tilt the way the lower part does.

BIG, YET LIGHT
The toco toucan's enormous beak is mostly air inside, with a honeycomblike texture. So it is lightweight, easily moved, and can grasp a single small berry.

SWISHING
The avocet swishes its bent beak in shallow water and mud to find food.

CRACKING
A scarlet macaw's stout beak cracks nuts with great force.

FILTERING
A flamingo's beak has ridges inside to filter small prey from water.

STABBING

The sharp talons of raptors (birds of prey), like the osprey or fish hawk, jab deeply into prey, even slippery, wriggling victims such as fish.

CLIMBING

Woodpeckers jab their sharp claws into the tree trunk for a firm grip while pecking.

PERCHING

Perching birds like this cut-throat finch wrap their toes around narrow twigs.

FEET

Most birds have four toes on each foot. Each toe is tipped with a claw. Birds that spend much time in trees have sharp claws that dig into the bark, while ground-dwelling birds have rounded, blunt claws. A bird of prey's large, sharp, curved claws are called talons. They are suited more for stabbing into and catching prey than for walking and perching.

GETTING A GRIP

In most birds, muscles in the legs are connected to the toes by long, stringlike tendons. The rear leg muscles (red) pull the front and rear toes together so they "lock" around a perch. A muscle at the front (blue) pulls the toes apart to release the grip.

GRIPPING

Parrots use one foot like a hand to hold seeds, while the beak removes the shells.

PADDLING

The webbed feet of waterfowl, such as this white-faced duck, are good paddles for swimming.

SPREADING

The very long toes of the lesser moorhen spread its weight, so it can walk on floating leaves.

COLORS AND CAMOUFLAGE

Some birds show all the colors of the rainbow, while others are so dull that they are hardly noticed. And some birds are both bright and dull—but at different times of year.

SHINING BRIGHT
In the breeding season, some birds molt their dull, winter feathers for new, brightly colored ones. This happens mainly in males so they can impress females and have a chance to mate.

DULL AND DREARY
Many birds are drab, especially out of the breeding season. They are usually flecked with shades of dark green, dark brown, and black. These patterns are for camouflage—blending in with the surroundings so the bird is less noticed by predators and enemies.

PINK FOOD
Flamingoes feed on tiny water creatures, such as shrimp. The birds take in their prey's pinkish coloring substances, or pigments, called carotenoids. These make a flamingo's feathers pink.

IT'S ME!
Each European bee eater has a slightly different color pattern. This may help partners recognize each other in the busy nesting colony.

METALLIC
Birds like the glossy starling shine with glinting colors, as if made of polished metal. This is called iridescence.

CRESTS

Birds like cockatoos, lories, and turacos (right) have head crests that usually lie flat on the neck. When the bird is excited or worried, the feathers rise up and fan out to reveal the crest's color and pattern.

A SPLASH OF COLOR

Some birds have bold color patterns with large patches that stand out clearly. These patterns help to break up the bird's outline so its overall shape is less recognizable to enemies. This is known as disruptive coloration.

CHANGES THROUGH THE SEASONS

In the far north, the landscape is green and brown with plants and soil in summer, but white with ice and snow in winter. Ptarmigans molt their plumage twice yearly to fit in with these changes. They are mottled brown in summer and mostly white in winter.

BRIGHT MALE

In spring, the male wood duck grows his bright breeding plumage. The female is more camouflaged, because she will have the task of raising chicks.

LIKE A REED

In camouflage, a bird's color, as well as its behavior, is important. The mottled brown bittern merges with the reeds. It also points its beak up and sways like a reed in the wind.

STUMP IMPERSONATOR

The potoo catches insect food at night. By day, it sits perfectly still on a tree, looking exactly like an old broken stump.

CALLS AND SONGS

Birds use sounds more than any other animals. They make two main types of sounds. Calls are relatively short and simple, like a "tic," and usually have a single purpose, such as warning of danger. Songs tend to be longer, more tuneful, and more varied.

WHY BIRDS SING

Brief calls like an alarm signal are often quite similar among several species of birds. So if one bird spots a predator, such as a cat, and gives the alarm call, all the birds in the area recognize its purpose and are warned of the danger.

Songs tend to differ between different species, and vary even between individuals of one species. There are several types of songs for different purposes, such as attracting a mate at breeding time or when competing for partners or territory.

FLOCKS

Birds that live in groups, like geese, often make regular quiet calls so that each flock member knows where the others are.

STRONG SINGERS

Vireos like this Bell's vireo (below) are well-known for their loud and persistent songs, especially during breeding time.

SONG OF THE NIGHT

The nightingale's famous song has many variations in tone, volume, and melody. It is often delivered in the quiet of the night.

This grouse has a balloonlike bag of skin on the chin or throat. This blows up and vibrates, or resonates, to make the bird's low, deep call much louder.

TRUMPETERS

We often describe birdcalls and songs by comparing them to musical instruments. Cranes, such as the blue crane, tend to make trumpeting sounds.

DAWN AND DUSK

Many birds sing most often and most loudly just after dawn, in what is called the "dawn chorus." They also sing before dusk. Usually, this is to announce that they occupy a territory—a patch of land or area where the bird lives, feeds, and breeds. A territory is vital for survival. So a bird defends its territory and chases away intruders with displays such as flapping wings and sharp, aggressive calls.

THE SYRINX

Our own voice box, or larynx, is in the neck. A bird's voice box, called the syrinx, is in the chest, at the base of the windpipe. Muscles alter its shape to change the pitch and tone of the sound made by air pushed out of the lungs.

Windpipe

Sound waves in syrinx

Muscles

Air chamber

Air from lungs

MIMICS

Lyre birds (above left), budgerigars (above right), mynahs, and parrots mimic, or copy, sounds such as our own speech, music, and machinery. Why they do so is unclear.

21

LONG-DISTANCE TRAVELERS

The power of flight means that birds are the greatest of all animal migrants. Many make immense journeys, usually twice yearly, between their summer and winter areas.

CANADA TO MEXICO
Canada geese breed in northern North America and fly south in V-formation to the Gulf of Mexico in autumn.

REASONS FOR MIGRATION

In the far north of the world, summer brings extra sunlight and a short period of plentiful plant growth. However, winters are long, dark, and icy. With their ability to fly fast and far, birds such as geese and waders are able to travel to northern areas in spring. The birds spend summer with few competitors for food and breeding space. As conditions change in autumn, the migrants return south for winter in warmer, more sheltered regions.

TROPICAL WINTER

Other birds migrate between the temperate lands of Europe, Asia, and North America in summer and tropical regions such as Africa, India, and Central America in winter. They include swallows, swifts, and warblers. In another type of migration, some birds fly to the upper regions of high mountains for summer and return to sheltered valleys for winter.

A GROUP TRIP
On long journeys, many birds, such as these stilts, travel in flocks. They gain safety in numbers from attack by birds of prey, and they also have less chance of getting lost.

ENDLESS SUMMER

Common terns migrate many thousands of miles each year. Their cousin the arctic tern is the world's greatest migrant, flying 18,600 miles (30,000 km) or more yearly. It spends summer in the Arctic and winter in the Antarctic.

TINY MIGRANT

The ruby-throated hummingbird is among the smallest migrants. It travels 527 miles (850 km) nonstop from southern Florida to the Yucatan Peninsula in Mexico.

SIGN OF AUTUMN

Gathering flocks of birds ready to migrate, like barn swallows, signal cold weather is just ahead.

FINDING THEIR WAY

How do birds find their way on these long journeys? Some use clues like the position of the sun, moon, and stars in the sky. Or they learn to recognize landmarks such as mountains and rivers. Recent research shows that some birds have tiny specks of the metal iron in their brain and eyes. Iron is affected by Earth's natural magnetic field, so these birds may navigate using a "built-in" magnetic compass.

MIGRATION AT WALKING PACE

Penguins are flightless birds of the far south around Antarctica. The female emperor penguin lays one egg and leaves this with her male partner to keep warm. Then she treks across the ice to the sea, which may be many miles away. After several weeks, she returns well-fed to take over care of the chick.

BIRD COURTSHIP

When birds get together to breed, they try to show how healthy and fit they are to impress their possible partners. This is the basis of courtship.

CHOOSE ME
Each peacock (male peafowl) fans and rattles his amazing "eyed" tail feathers to show the female that he is the best choice as a mate.

FIT PARENTS
Courtship can include visual displays such as spreading feathers, calls and songs, and actions like "dancing" or acrobatic flights. Such behavior allows a bird to check that a partner is of the same species, of the opposite sex, and healthy. This gives the best chance of producing strong young.

DANCING COUPLE
Cranes are famous for courting "dances" in which the female and male jump, bow their heads, and flap their wings. The displays strengthen the pair's bond, helping them stay together.

INCREDIBLE DISPLAY
The bird world's most amazing displays are by birds of paradise, from Southeast Asia and Australia. Males spread and shake plumed feathers, sing loudly, dance, and hang upside down. Females are dull in color for camouflage.

BALLOON CHIN

The male magnificent frigatebird has a loose pouch of bright red throat skin. When courting, he noisily fills it with air like a balloon. This signal attracts the female to the site that he has chosen for their nest.

A GOOD BREEDING PLACE

Certain birds will only choose a breeding partner who has a territory. Occupying and defending a territory shows that a bird is healthy and able to survive well. The territory is also a relatively safe place to feed and rear young, free from competition with others.

SHORT- AND LONG-TERM

Most smaller birds live for only a few years. They choose a new breeding partner each year. Larger birds, such as swans, may live for 30 years or more. They have the same breeding partner year after year. This is known as forming a permanent pair bond and "mating for life."

AT THE LEK

Some birds, like the prairie chicken (above left), carry out courtship displays at a lek (above). This is a traditional site where the males gather to display as females watch.

MAKING AN IMPRESSION

Male bowerbirds do not have especially bright feathers or elaborate songs. Instead, they build bowers. A bower is usually made from twigs and leaves, perhaps decorated with colorful petals, pebbles, and shells. Each bowerbird species has its own bower design. The bower attracts the female to mate. She then leaves to make a separate nest.

Satin bowerbird with female in his bower

NESTS AND EGGS

Cups, domes, cones, balls, piles of sticks—birds build nests of almost every shape and design. The nest is where the eggs are laid. In some birds, the female makes the nest and sits on the eggs, or incubates them, to keep them warm. Sometimes both parents take part.

SIMPLE NEST
Most gulls make simple nests from twigs or whatever is available— even bits of string and plastic.

NEST-BUILDING SKILLS
Like many kinds of bird behavior, such as searching for food or courtship, nest-building is built-in, or instinctive. A bird is born knowing how to make its nest. Even so, early attempts may be poor. The bird learns details by practice and experience.

BUILDING MATERIALS
Nests are built from materials available in the habitat. Many smaller songbirds in woods, parks, and gardens use stems, twigs, and leaves, perhaps with a lining of moss or animal fur. But seaweed may be used on the shore, or mud in scrubland.

WOVEN NEST
Weaver birds, such as this masked weaver, construct intricate nests of grasses, stems, and leaves twined together. Some weavers use their nests all year for shelter and rest.

NO NEST
The white-fronted plover lays its eggs in a scrape in shore sand. Camouflage keeps the eggs safe.

PRISON NEST

Most hornbills, like the grey hornbill below, nest in tree holes. The male fills the opening with mud, except for a small hole. He passes food through this to the female inside.

WEB NEST

Paradise flycatchers use the sticky threads from spiders' webs to bind their nests together. They incubate the eggs for 14 to 16 days.

HOW MANY EGGS?

The number of eggs that a bird lays in one batch is called the clutch size. It varies from one in some penguins, albatrosses, and the flightless kiwi of New Zealand, to more than 20 in North American bobwhites and garden blue tits.

HUGE NEST

Birds of prey, such as these ospreys, build the largest nests. The nests, which are great mounds of sticks and twigs, are often used year after year and are enlarged each time.

INSIDE AN EGG

Within the protective eggshell is a tiny embryo—the developing baby bird. It receives nourishment along blood vessels from the yolk. Ostriches lay the largest eggs, and bee hummingbirds the tiniest (shown here life-size).

Eggs of hummingbird (left) and ostrich (behind and outside)

Embryo Yolk Blood supply

Air space

Albumin (egg white)

TREE-HOLE NEST

Holes in tree trunks are prized nesting sites for screech owls. Out of the breeding season, the hole is an owl's daytime roost.

BRINGING UP BABY BIRDS

S ome newly hatched chicks are
 helpless, without feathers and
unable to see. Others can walk
and run in hours, but it takes a
while before they are able to fly.

BEST PARENTS
Birds rival mammals as the animal
world's most caring parents. They feed
and protect their chicks with unceasing
energy. In many small songbirds, both
parents look after the young. In
other species, it is the female's
task. The ostrich is unusual—
the male takes the lead in
chick care.

STILL AT HOME
*Egret chicks stay in
the nest for about
six weeks after
hatching.*

PARENT ON GUARD
*Birds of prey, like the
African goshawk, fiercely
protect their chicks and will
swoop on, flap at, peck, and
scratch intruders.*

KEEPING WARM
*Young chicks, like these
boobies, are at first covered
with soft, fluffy down
feathers to keep them warm.*

PARENTAL CARE

Swiftlet chicks (above left) totally depend on their parents. The woodcock chick (above right) can run, but sits still and relies on camouflage when danger threatens.

HELPLESS OR DEVELOPED

Chicks born in safe, secure nests tend to be less developed. They are known as nidicolous and need weeks of care and feeding. More developed, or nidifugous, chicks leave the nest soon after hatching and quickly learn to feed themselves. However, they do not fledge, or start to fly, until they molt their soft, fluffy down for proper flight feathers.

FEEDING CHICKS

Most birds feed their young on animals rather than plant material. The kittiwake swallows fish and other prey at sea. At the nest, it brings the swallowed food back up for the chicks to eat.

CRECHE

Penguin chicks gather into groups, called creches, while their parents feed out at sea.

BROOD PARASITES

The common cuckoo is known as a "brood parasite." It lays its 10 to 15 eggs in the nests of other birds, usually one egg per nest. When the egg hatches, the large cuckoo chick pushes out the other eggs and chicks. The nest owners, who are usually smaller birds like warblers, dunnocks, or pipits, do not seem to notice the chick is not their own. They feed it, and the young cuckoo soon grows far larger than them.

Cuckoo chick and warbler foster parent

FOLLOW THE MOTHER

Young waterfowl like these Canada geese follow the first large moving object they see— usually the mother.

FLIGHTLESS BIRDS

Several groups of birds are unable to fly—but their other abilities make up for this lack. The ostrich and emu run very fast, while penguins swim and dive far below the waves.

THE RATITES

The larger types of flightless birds are called the ratites. In order of decreasing size, they include the ostrich of the African desert, the emu of the Australian outback, three kinds of cassowary from the forests of New Guinea and Australia, and two types of rhea from South American grasslands. Ratites feed on plant matter like leaves and seeds, as well as worms, grubs, and small vertebrate animals.

BIGGEST BIRD
The ostrich is by far the biggest bird, up to 8.25 feet (2.5 m) tall and 330 pounds (150 kg) in weight. It is also the fastest creature on two legs, running at speeds of 46.5 miles (75 km) per hour.

WANDERING FLOCKS
Ostrich flocks wander widely across the African desert, scrub, and grassland. In the breeding season, males may fight each other for the females with dangerous kicks and pecks.

MANY MATES
When breeding season begins, the male common rhea makes loud booming noises to attract females. He may mate with 10 or more. Together, the females lay 50-plus eggs in a scraped-out nest.

GOING FISHING

Emperor penguins can dive deeper than 550 yards (500 m).

WADDLING PENGUIN

The Magellanic penguin lives along the southwest coast of South America, as far north as Brazil. It nests in a long burrow.

PENGUINS IN ICY SEAS

Most of the 17 species of penguins live on islands and icebergs around the great southern continent of Antarctica. They flap their flipper-shaped wings up and down to "fly" quickly through the water.

Penguins eat fish, squid, and other sea creatures. The bird's thick coat of feathers and a fatty layer under the skin called blubber keep it warm in the freezing seas and biting winds.

SHY AND SECRETIVE

New Zealand's main flightless birds are three types of kiwis. They have no tails, soft plumelike feathers, and very long beaks with nostrils at the end to sniff out soil-dwelling prey.

NO NEED TO FLY

In the remote Galapagos Islands of the Pacific, there were no large predators. So the Galapagos cormorant had no need to flap away from danger—and lost the power of flight. It dives into the sea and swims expertly after fish and squid.

EMU PESTS

Emus can breed year-round if conditions are good. When numbers rise, they raid farm crops and can be serious pests.

31

SEABIRDS

The open oceans are the world's largest habitat, teeming with fish, shellfish, squid, and tiny floating creatures and plants called plankton. More than 1,000 kinds of birds live and feed here. Some stay out at sea for months on end.

OCEANIC WANDERERS

The birds that live farthest out at sea are about 80 species of albatrosses and petrels. The wandering albatross's 10-foot (3-m) wingspan is the largest of any bird. The albatross soars for days without flapping. Petrels are smaller and include Wilson's storm petrel. This sooty-black bird is one of the most numerous of all birds, numbering in the tens of millions.

TAKING A REST

Most seabirds have plentiful oil-producing glands in their skin. As a seabird rests and dries after fishing, it spreads the oil over its feathers to keep them smooth and waterproof.

RUNNING TAKE-OFF

Large seabirds, like this albatross, usually take off by jumping or running into the wind. This gives them enough speed for their long wings to provide lift.

SOUNDS OF THE SEASHORE

Gulls like these kelp gulls are mostly noisy, squabbling shore scavengers. Some kinds, such as herring gulls, have greatly increased their numbers by feeding on our rubbish, scraps, and leftovers.

CASPIAN TERN

This tern feeds in rivers and lakes, as well as oceans. It eats chicks and eggs and robs other birds of food.

OPEN SEA AND CLOSE TO SHORE

The nine species of gannets and boobies also feed out at sea, although they come to land regularly to rest. With their wings folded back, they dive from heights of 33 yards (30 m) or more. Then they swim fast after fish and other prey.

The 90 species of mainly white terns and gulls are familiar seabirds around the world. Terns are small and graceful. They swoop down to dip at the surface or dive beneath for fish. Gulls are bigger and feed chiefly along shores.

NESTS ON COASTS

Many seabirds nest in groups, or colonies, on rocky cliffs and ledges where few predators can reach (right). Horned puffins (above) lay single eggs between rocks or boulders.

SKIMMING THE WAVES

Skimmers are coastal birds of the Americas. The lower part of the beak is longer than the upper. It skims through the water to snap up small surface prey like fish.

FISHING THE SHOALS

Seabirds often gather in enormous flocks above shoals of plentiful fish or squid. Common Manx shearwaters skim the surface, dipping their beaks to grab food. They also dive in after prey. These shearwaters, which are a type of petrel, travel hundreds of miles to find food.

WATERBIRDS

The waterfowl bird group includes more than 140 kinds of ducks, geese, and swans. But many other birds live in the freshwater habitats of lakes, rivers, and swampy wetlands—from fast-flying kingfishers to slow-wading herons.

DUCKS AND GEESE

Waterfowl have stout bodies and short legs with webbed feet for paddling and swimming. Their beaks are broad, flat, and blunt-tipped. When feeding at the surface or in shallow water, ducks and geese often "dabble." They quickly open and close their beaks. This stirs the water and mud, allowing the bird to gather small bits of plant food or small water creatures.

In most waterfowl, especially ducks, the males are brightly colored at breeding time. They quack and peck each other to win the attention of females. However, the dull-colored female raises the chicks.

CHIN BAG

The brown pelican's loose chin skin fills with water like a balloon when the bird feeds. The pelican then expels the water, keeping the food in its beak.

BOTTOMS UP

Some waterfowl, like this northern pintail duck, "up-end." They tip the body forward so the tail points straight up. Then they reach down to feed underwater.

STANDSTILL

The typical hunting method of herons, such as the purple heron of Africa (left), is to wade very slowly or stand perfectly still. Eventually, prey swims past, and the heron grabs it with lightning speed—even if it's a lizard or snake.

SPEAR FISHER

The snakebird uses its feet to swim fast underwater. It stabs fish with is spear-shaped beak. After feeding, it dries its wings.

TALL WADERS

The 60 or so kinds of herons and egrets are tall and slim. They have long legs for wading in shallow water, long necks, and dagger-shaped beaks. A heron does not usually stab its victims, such as fish or frogs, but grabs them with its beak.

Other tall waders of mainly freshwater habitats include five species of flamingoes with beaks that filter small prey from water and 17 kinds of storks.

RAILS

The rail family includes 130 species of crakes, moorhens, coots, and gallinules. The purple gallinule (above) eats worms, snails, dragonflies, and other small creatures, as well as water plants. Most rails are very shy and seldom seen.

FEEDING FLOCK

Flamingoes are found in huge, dense flocks that fly, feed, and breed together.

"DECORATIVE" WATERBIRDS

Many types of waterbirds, especially waterfowl, have been taken by people to new regions to brighten up ponds and lakes. The black swan came originally from Australia, where it is an emblem of the state of Western Australia. It now lives in dozens of other countries as far apart as Sweden and New Zealand. In some areas, it has become a pest.

Black swans have white-tipped wing feathers.

GREAT HUNTERS

A sharp and fierce-looking hooked beak, large eyes, and pointed claws or talons—these features signify a bird of prey. The main two groups of predatory birds are raptors, with about 300 different species, and owls, with 150 to 200 species.

NOT BALD
The bald eagle's head may look featherless at a distance, but the feathers are white. This eagle's huge wings reach 8 feet (2.4 m) across.

KILLERS BY DAY
The raptor group includes eagles, hawks, falcons, and harriers. It also includes vultures and condors, which are more scavengers than predators. Raptors hunt by day using their amazing eyesight. An eagle can spot a rabbit 10 times farther away than where we could see it.

HARPY EAGLE
Probably the biggest eagle, this South American hunter eats large forest animals like monkeys.

GROUND HUNTERS
A few birds of prey stalk their victims on the ground, rather than swooping in from the air. The caracara (inset) of the Americas eats any animal food from beetles to dead sheep and turtles. The African secretary bird (left) can peck and stamp snakes to death.

GREAT HORNED OWL

Owls have both excellent sight and hearing, and they use both senses to find prey. The "horns" of horned owls are not horns, but tufts of feathers.

FALCONRY

For centuries people have kept trained falcons and other raptors, like this hawk. Some birds catch food for their owners; others are only for show.

PREDATORS AND PREY

Usually bigger birds of prey hunt bigger victims. In Australia, the huge wedge-tailed eagle can carry away a small wallaby. The black-thighed and Bornean falconets of Southeast Asia are only 6 inches (15 centimeters) from beak to tail tip. They feed on insects like small dragonflies and beetles.

The little kestrel hunts little sparrows.

KILLERS AT NIGHT

Most owls hunt in twilight or darkness. However, when they have hungry chicks to feed, they may be active in daytime. The owl's eyes are so huge, taking up half the head, that they cannot swivel to look around. So the owl has a very flexible neck. It can turn its head in half a circle either direction to look directly behind.

Some experts recognize about 140 species of owls. Others say there are more than 200. This depends on whether some widespread kinds, such as the barn owl, are considered a single species or many different ones in different regions. Indeed, the barn owl is one of the world's most wide-raging land birds. It is found on every continent except Antarctica.

FEEDING VULTURES

Vultures, such as the king vulture (right), soar high looking for dead or dying victims. The African white-backed vultures (above) are battling with hyenas over a carcass.

FOREST AND WOODLAND BIRDS

More than half of all bird species live in woods and forests—mainly tropical rain forests. They use trees for feeding, perching, roosting, nesting on branches and in holes—in fact, for every need of life.

WIDE DIET

Many woodland birds, like the blackbird, eat both animals and plants. The medium-sized beak is good for eating berries, seeds, insects, and worms.

HELPFUL EATERS

Other birds eat specific kinds of foods. In honeycreepers, sunbirds, and some hummingbirds, the beak is long and thin, almost like a needle. It probes deep into tree flowers to sip sweet, sticky nectar. As birds do this, their feathers pick up tiny pollen grains. The birds then visit other trees, carrying the pollen. This enables the flowers to develop fruits and seeds.

NUT HACKER

The nuthatch's name is a version of the term "nut hack." This bird (left) wedges nuts into cracks in tree bark. Then it pecks them hard to break through the shell.

BIRD BRAINS?

A "bird brain" may be stupid. But some birds show skilled behavior, such as tool use. The woodpecker finch of the Galapagos Islands uses a cactus spine to probe into holes and remove grubs. The New Caledonian crow uses a sharp leaf, stem, or hook-shaped twig to do the same. The Egyptian vulture picks up stones and drops them on eggs to break the shells and get at the meal inside. In captivity, birds such as parrots can learn many complicated tricks, which include counting up to five or six.

Galapagos woodpecker finch

RAT-AT-AT-AT

A young bearded woodpecker (left) from Africa shows its typical pecking posture. Its feet are spread and the stiff-feathered tail is used as a rear support.

PECKING WOOD

Among tree-dwellers are more than 200 species of woodpeckers, including wrynecks and piculets. Their sharp-clawed toes grip bark firmly, and the tail acts as a strut or support as the woodpecker leans back to hammer bark. These birds peck to find food such as grubs, dig out nesting holes, and make drumming sounds that warn of territorial ownership or attract a mate.

NORTHERN WOODS

Crossbills are finches of the conifer forests covering northern lands. They use the crossed-over beak to pry and twist seeds from pine and fir cones.

TROPICAL COLOR

Parrots and macaws, like these blue-and-gold macaws, feed in squawking flocks on fruits and seeds.

EXPERT FLIERS

Hummingbirds beat their wings up to 100 times each second and can fly backward. These are Allen's hummingbirds, male (left) and female.

NOISY CLIMBER

The African purple-crested lourie (a type of turaco) prefers clambering among branches to flying. It searches for figs and other fruits, plus some insects.

GRASSLAND AND DESERT BIRDS

In dry grassland, scrub, and deserts, there are few trees for perching and nesting. Many birds tend to feed and nest on the ground among the grass stems, or they flutter between the low bushes and shrubs.

FLOWER FEEDERS
Anna's hummingbirds (male on left, female to right) survive in dense shrubland, but find more flowers in parks and gardens.

INSECT FOOD
Wagtails, like the African pied wagtail, forage on the ground near large grazers such as zebras. The birds snap up the insects that the grazers disturb.

WALKERS AND RUNNERS
Big flightless birds, such as the ostrich, emu, and rhea, are found in dry habitats. Many smaller kinds of birds here can fly, but prefer to walk or run. They have strong legs and large feet and scratch in the soil for seeds and grubs. However, flight is very useful to reach water, which could be tens of miles away.

GAMBEL'S QUAIL
Most quails are small members of the pheasant family. They only fly when in danger.

RED-CRESTED BUSTARD
Large, sturdy bustards are among the heaviest fliers. They stride across the grassland looking for seeds and insects.

SPEEDY RUNNER
The roadrunner (above left) of southwestern North America is one of the fastest birds on the ground. It races along at more than 15 miles (24 km) per hour.

THE "FEATHERED LOCUST"

The red-billed quelea of Africa, a type of weaver bird, is one of the most numerous wild birds—and most destructive. Huge flocks destroy large areas of grain crops. Queleas are viewed as feathered versions of the insects called locusts, which also form huge swarms.

The sky darkens with red-billed queleas.

NOISY WOODPECKER
The gila woodpecker of southwestern North America makes a loud repetitive "yip" call and pecks on walls and roofs.

ALWAYS ON THE GO

Many scrub and desert birds are nomadic. They wander in large flocks, feeding on the plants and insects that appear after a rare rainfall. As soon as they have eaten all the food in an area, the birds continue their search. Breeding follows the rain whenever it falls, rather than occurring at the same time each year.

DESERT "TREE"
In American deserts, tall cacti like the saguaro offer birds places to nest as well as vantage points to perch and look for food.

OUT FROM UNDER GROUND
Tree holes are rare in grasslands and deserts, so burrowing owls nest in ground holes instead. Here, chicks wait for a parent to bring food.

SAVING BIRDS

Wildlife experts estimate that more than 1,000 bird species are at serious risk of dying out forever. Almost all cases are due to human activity, from loss of habitat to shooting for "sport."

HABITAT DESTROYED
Tropical forests are the richest habitats for birds and other wildlife. But they are also disappearing most quickly.

PLASTIC MENACE
Plastic litter does not rot, or biodegrade. It can kill birds and other animals many years later.

MODERN FARMING
Farmers spray chemicals to kill insects. But the chemicals affect other creatures, too, many of which are food for birds.

HABITAT LOSS
Around the world, the greatest overall threat to birds and other wildlife is habitat loss. This happens when humans take over natural places and convert them to areas such as farmland, planted forests, roads, houses, factories, or leisure parks. It is of little use trying to save individual species of birds or other animals if there are no natural habitats for them to live in.

CAGED-BIRD TRADE

It is illegal to capture many kinds of birds. But enforcing the law is difficult in remote areas. Parrots have suffered greatly in this way.

FAILURE AND SUCCESS

Further threats include capture for the pet trade or for valuable feathers, and poisoning or shooting. This sometimes happens by accident when another animal, which is a pest, is the target.

The last two Hawaiian crows in the wild disappeared in 2002. Some of these crows have been saved in captivity. The plan is to breed them so they can be released, or reintroduced, back into the wild. About one-quarter of threatened bird species are being helped in this way.

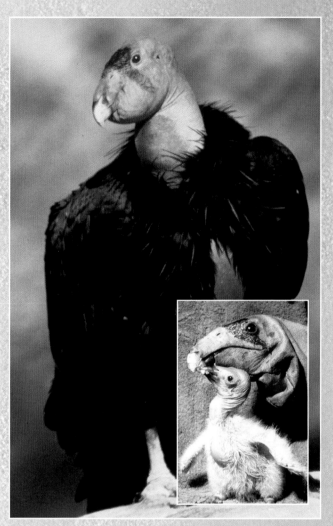

SLOWLY RECOVERING

Californian condors were shot and poisoned for many years. By 1982 there were only about 25 left. Most were collected to breed in captivity, where chicks are fed using a special parentlike glove (inset). Now their numbers exceed 200.

NEW HOMES

We can all help birds by simple actions such as placing nest boxes and providing food in harsh conditions. But saving a whole species is a complex task, needing support and money.

LONG GONE

Before Europeans arrived in North America, the passenger pigeon was perhaps the most common bird in the region, numbering in the millions. By 1914, there was just one left, called Martha. She died in the Cincinnati Zoo on September 1st of that year.

ANIMAL CLASSIFICATION

The animal kingdom can be split into two main groups, vertebrates (with a backbone) and invertebrates (without a backbone). From these two main groups, scientists classify, or sort, animals further based on their shared characteristics.

The six main groupings of animals, from the most general to the most specific, are: phylum, class, order, family, genus, and species. This system was created by Carolus Linnaeus.

To see how this system works, follow the example of how human beings are classified in the vertebrate group and how earthworms are classified in the invertebrate group.

ANIMAL KINGDOM

VERTEBRATE	INVERTEBRATE
PHYLUM: Chordata	**PHYLUM:** Annelida
CLASS: Mammals	**CLASS:** Oligochaeta
ORDER: Primates	**ORDER:** Haplotaxida
FAMILY: Hominids	**FAMILY:** Lumbricidae
GENUS: *Homo*	**GENUS:** *Lumbricus*
SPECIES: *sapiens*	**SPECIES:** *terrestris*

There are more than 30 groups of phyla. The nine most common are listed below along with their common name.

Annelida (SEGMENTED WORMS)

Arthropoda (ARTHROPODS)

CHORDATA (CHORDATES)

Cnidaria (CNIDARIANS)

Echinodermata (ECHINODERMS)

Mollusca (MOLLUSKS)

Nematoda (ROUNDWORMS)

Platyhelminthes (FLATWORMS)

Porifera (SPONGES)

This book highlights animals from the Chordata phylum. Follow the example below to learn how scientists classify the *sulfuratus*, or keel-billed toucan.

VERTEBRATE

PHYLUM: Chordata

CLASS: Aves

ORDER: Piciformes

FAMILY: Ramphastidae

GENUS: *Ramphastos*

SPECIES: *sulfuratus*

Keel-billed toucan
(sulfuratus)

GLOSSARY

BLUBBER
A thick layer of fat just under the skin, as in penguins, which keeps in body warmth

CAMOUFLAGE
The disguising of an animal by the way it is colored and patterned to blend or merge with its surroundings

CLOACA
The hole on bird's body for getting rid of wastes as well as secreting sperm or eggs

CLUTCH
A group or batch of eggs all laid by a female bird at about the same time

COLD-BLOODED
Having a body temperature that varies with the temperature of its surroundings, so an animal is cool in cold weather and warm in hot sunny weather

CONTOUR FEATHERS
Feathers that cover a bird's body, giving a smooth surface for flight; they also provide protection, coloration, and keep in body warmth

CROP
In a bird's digestive system, a baglike body part or organ for storage of food that's just been swallowed, before it passes to the next part, the gizzard

DISRUPTIVE COLORATION
Bold colors and patterns that help to break up an animal's outline so its overall body shape is less recognizable to enemies

DOWN FEATHERS
Soft, fluffy feathers, usually found on the body under the contour feathers, which keep in body warmth

EVOLUTION
The change in living things through time as they become better adapted or suited to their surroundings or environment

FLIGHT FEATHERS
Large broad-vaned feathers on a bird's wings, giving a smooth air-proof surface for lift and control during flight

FOLLICLES
Tiny pits or pockets in the skin from which a bird's feathers grow

GIZZARD
In a bird's digestive system, a muscular part, or organ, that grinds and mashes swallowed food; also called the stomach

HABITAT
A particular type of surroundings or environment where plants and animals live, such as a desert, mountainside, pond, or seashore

INCUBATE
When a parent bird sits on the eggs in the nest to keep them protected and warm, allowing the embryos (babies) inside to develop properly

KERATIN
A hard, light, tough substance that forms the beak, feathers, scales, and claws of a bird

LEK
A small area where several male birds display to attract females at breeding time

MANDIBLES
The upper and lower jawbones attached to the skull; in birds, they are covered by the upper and lower parts of the beak

MIGRATION
A regular long journey by an animal, usually at the same time each year, to avoid harsh conditions such as cold or drought

MOLT
To cast off, or shed, a body covering; when birds lose their old feathers and grow a new set, usually twice each year

PASSERINES
The largest subgroup of birds, with over half of all species, including familiar songbirds, perching birds, and garden birds

SYRINX
A part at the base of a bird's windpipe, just above the lungs, which makes the sounds of the bird's calls and songs

TALONS
Large, sharp, curved toe claws, found on the feet of most birds of prey such as hawks and eagles

TERRITORY
An area where an animal lives, and which it defends against others of its kind; some territories are used only for feeding, some for breeding, and some for both

WARM-BLOODED
Using the energy in food to keep the body at a constant warm temperature at all times, even if the temperature of the surroundings varies greatly; the main groups of warm-blooded animals are mammals and birds

FURTHER RESOURCES

AT THE LIBRARY
Burnie, David. *Bird*. New York: DK Children, 2004.

Holmes, Thom and Laurie. *Feathered Dinosaurs: The Origins of Birds*. Berkeley Heights, N.J.: Enslow, 2002.

Laubach, Christyna, Rene Laubach, and Charles W. G. Smith. *Raptor! A Kid's Guide to Birds of Prey*. North Adams, Mass.: Storey Books, 2002.

Salmansohn, Pete, and Stephen W. Kress. *Saving Birds: Heroes Around the World*. Gardiner, Maine: Tilbury House, 2003.

ON THE WEB
For more information on *birds,* use FactHound to track down Web sites related to this book.

1. Go to *www.facthound.com*
2. Type in a search word related to this book or this book ID: 0756512514
3. Click on the *Fetch It* button

FactHound will find the best Web sites for you.

INDEX